MW01226816

PROGRAMME GUIDE COMPUTER SCIENCE AT CAMBRIDGE

UniAdmissions

Copyright © 2021 *UniAdmissions*. All rights reserved.

ISBN 978-1-913683-73-3

No part of this publication may be reproduced or transmitted in any form or by any means, electronic or mechanical, including photocopying, recording, or by any information retrieval system without prior written permission of the publisher. This publication may not be used in conjunction with or to support any commercial undertaking without the prior written permission of the publisher.

Published by *RAR Medical Services Limited*
www.uniadmissions.co.uk
books@uniadmissions.co.uk
Tel: +44 (0) 208 068 0438

This book is neither created nor endorsed by Cambridge University or Cambridge Assessment. The authors and publisher are not affiliated with Cambridge University. The information offered in this book is purely advisory and any advice given should be taken within this context. As such, the publishers and authors accept no liability whatsoever for the outcome of any applicant's interview performance, the outcome of any university applications or for any other loss. Although every precaution has been taken in the preparation of this book, the publisher and author assume no responsibility for errors or omissions of any kind. Neither is any liability assumed for damages resulting from the use of information contained herein. This does not affect your statutory rights.

Contents

Welcome to UniAdmissions

Thanks for booking your Programme with UniAdmissions and taking that vital first step towards optimizing your university application.

We'll do everything we can to help you achieve your dream place.

Who Are We?

UniAdmissions was founded by two Cambridge graduates because they fought through the overwhelming minefield that is applying for university. They couldn't find any useful resources to help them navigate it: thus, UniAdmissions was born and has been thriving since 2013!

Over the last decade, the competition for the most sought-after university places has been steadily increasing. This has led to the introduction of measures, such as Admissions Tests, to set candidates apart.

Just as we did, many students find this daunting and are confused by how to put together a winning application. This is where UniAdmissions come in.

We've supported hundreds of students with their applications to the most competitive universities and degrees. Over the years, we've built a very strong track record in getting students their dream offers – students enrolled with us are three times more likely to get their Cambridge place.

With over 1,000 expert Cambridge tutors, 24/7 support and world-class resources, you're in safe hands with your application.

How Your Programme Works

Once you book, you'll be assigned a dedicated Programme Manager. They will do everything they can to ensure your Programme runs smoothly.

You'll be introduced to your Programme Manager who will then match your specific requirements with tutors who are best suited to your needs. You'll also be sent over any resources that are included with your Programme.

You'll be given information about the tutors your Programme Manager has carefully selected for you, and the tutors will then contact you directly to arrange your first session. This will always be within 48 hours of your tutor being allocated.

Your Programme Managers

Your Programme Manager is your main point of contact as the Programme progresses.

They are fully briefed on your unique requirements by our Admissions Team and are committed to ensuring you receive expert tuition. They work closely alongside our tutors to ensure you get the most from your Programme.

If you have issues with any aspect of your Programme, they are here to help every step of the way. Their contact details are available below. You should reach out to your assigned Programme Manager with any queries you have.

Harmeet Ghai
Head of Programmes
harmeet@uniadmissions.co.uk
07397 903 890

BOOK A SESSION WITH THE TUTOR

COMPLETE ANY WORK ASSIGNED BY THE TUTOR

DISCUSS YOUR AIMS WITH YOUR TUTOR

IDENTIFY WEAKNESSES AND STRENGTHS

HAVE YOUR TUTORING SESSION

REVIEW SESSION FEEDBACK FROM TUTOR

Preparing for your First Session

You will be sent a Student Profile Form link to complete before your first session with your tutor - make sure to complete it in good time. Read through this Programme Guide and take a look at your resources so that you feel confident and comfortable navigating through them. Consider any areas of your application that you are finding more challenging and inform your tutor or your Programme Manager in advance so they can prepare material accordingly.

Additional Support included in your Programme

Your Admissions Consultant will have highlighted all the resources and support that is included in your Programme. Depending on your Programme these may include all or some of the resources below.

- Essay Marking
- Personal Statement Editing Service
- Intensive One Day Course(s)
- Online Courses
- All Relevant Paperback Books & eBooks
- Consultation with Our Professional Exam Coach
- Mock Interviews
- Enrichment Seminars

Important Note:

Don't worry if your Programme doesn't include absolutely everything mentioned in the list above. We tailor your programme based on your requirements and some things may not be covered in it. The important thing is that you prepare thoroughly, make full use of the resources provided, and follow the guidance given in this Programme Guide to maximise your chances of success. If you'd like to add anything to your Programme, please contact your Programme Manager.

What do you need to succeed?

Cambridge might seem like something mysterious and secret, especially for the sciences, and open only to people who speak fluent Latin and have a grade eight in harpsichord, but this couldn't be further from the truth. Most students are admitted from state schools, and the most common jobs for graduates are in teaching.

Similarly, getting into Cambridge isn't about knowing the secret signals or obeying the 'real rules' that only a few insiders know. It's about having a passion for your subject, outstanding A levels, a great reference, and shining in the interview. In fact, the single most predictive thing for getting in or not isn't where you went to school, what you said in your personal statement, or even what your reference says about you. It's how well you did in your GCSEs.

To take Cambridge as an example, they weigh the parts of your application on the following basis:

Factor	High	Medium	Low
GCSE (or equivalent) Grades	•		
A level (or equivalent) Predicted Grades	•		
UCAS Reference		•	
AS Module Grades (if taken)			•
UCAS personal statement			•

This is borne out by the data as well. Over the past three years, the average Cambridge applicant has had 7.2 A*s and 2.7 As at GCSE. The average offer holder though – that's the subset of applicants who actually get in – has applied with 8.6 A*s and 1.2 As. So, from a GCSE perspective, the difference between applying and getting in is turning an A into an A*, and a B into an A.

None of this means that you shouldn't be applying if your GCSEs are less than perfect though, as there is a huge amount of variation within this data. As universities put more emphasis on contextual admissions – taking into account each applicant's life and educational circumstances – the average GCSE grades of offer holders have fallen over the past three years, from 8.74 A*s and 1.19 As in 2017, to 8.35 A*s and 1.16 As in 2019.

And remember, these are mean averages. That means that around half of all applicants, and half of all offer holders, didn't do quite as well as these figures would suggest.

The most important thing to understand is that applying to Cambridge isn't mysterious or random. If your ambition is to study Computer Science, your path forward is quite simple. Get great GCSEs, be predicted straight As at A-level, and make sure that your UCAS reference and personal statement both show you in the best possible light. It might sound like a lot of work, but the important thing to understand is that all this is within your control. All you need to do is work hard, work smart, and focus on your goal. It's in your hands!

How hard is it to get in?

If you want to apply to Cambridge, you're going to need to be interested in probability. Knowing the difference between a 1% chance, a one in ten shot, and a sure thing is fundamental in life, especially if you like to play cards. It's also pretty useful to come into the university application process with your eyes open. If you've got mediocre GCSE results, barely cracked open a book outside of set texts in the past two years, and got a D in Maths, you're not going to get into any subject at Cambridge.

But this doesn't mean that only straight A* geniuses who've already founded and sold companies, raised millions for charity, or been nominated for the Nobel Peace Prize can get in. Who gets in, and what scores they get is all public information, so you can have a good idea of the odds you're up against. It's not an exact science but if you're closer to the profile of an offer holder than of an applicant, you're on the right track.

Computer Science at Cambridge – Average Applicants & Offer Holders

	Applicant	Offer Holder
Number	749	109
GCSE Scores	6A*s, 3As, 2 Bs	8A*s, 2A, 1B
Predicted A Levels	A*A*A	A*A*A*
CTMUA Maths Thinking	5.1	7.0
CTMUA Maths Reasoning	5.2	7.2
CSAT (where applicable)	45.4	68

What is studying Computer Science at Cambridge like?

This article was contributed by Anoushka Mazumdar, a tutor with UniAdmissions, and a second-year in Computer Science at Churchill College.

Course Structure

The Bachelor's course is a three year course (the three years are called Part IA, IB and II), but there is an optional integrated Master's with a fourth year (Part III). To gain admission to the Master's program you have to achieve a first class at your third year final exams.

The full range of courses and options is available online, but some of the main differences between the three years are described below.

First Year (Part IA)

There are four papers taken at the end of this year, one of which is the Maths Paper. The lectures for this Maths paper are taken alongside the Natural Sciences Tripos, and there is an option to take Maths A or Maths B. Maths B is aimed at those who studied Further Maths at A level, with the lectures moving at a slightly faster pace, and more content being covered. This will give you a greater choice of questions to answer in the final exam, but both Maths A and Maths B students take the same final paper. The other three papers are from the Computer Science Tripos and are all assessed by written exam at the end of the year. There are no course choices this year.

Second Year (Part IB)

There are four papers in the final exam, all for Computer Science, at the end of the year. All students must attend all lectures, but there is a choice of topics to answer questions on in the exam. There is also a group project that runs in the second term (Lent term) where students are in a group of 6-7, and work with a client for two months to deliver a product or service according to their specifications. This aims to give students more practical experience and learn teamwork skills.

Third Year (Part II)

Whilst this year has results based on final examinations, you are also required to complete an independent Part II project on a topic of your choice. You will have a supervisor to give you advice throughout the project, and will produce a dissertation by the end. The mark from your Part II project will count towards your final class for third year. There is also a choice of two optional modules to take, which are examined at the end of the module, rather than in the final exam.

Assessment and Practical Work

The degree classes (1st, 2.I, 2.II, 3rd, fail) are awarded based on end of year examinations (slightly different for 3rd year, detailed above). There is also practical coursework (called ticks) to be completed throughout the degree, for the courses that require it. If you do not pass a practical then marks will be deducted from your final exam score; however everyone typically passes all of their practical work.

What is it like to Study there?

Lectures

I found the first year particularly challenging, since I came with barely any background knowledge in Computer Science. However, by the end of the first year everyone is brought up to the same level. Currently as a second year, I have found that an understanding of the course content comes much more quickly. Almost all lectures happen in the morning (most after 10am) with a few running into the afternoon. In the first year we had 11 lectures a week (including Maths). This second year we have had 13 per week but fewer towards the end of the 2nd term to allow for time to work on the group project. Most first year lectures are located away from the Computer Lab, but from second year onwards almost all lectures will be in the Lab in West Cambridge – this might be a factor to consider for college choice, depending on how much you like cycling.

Practical Work

In my opinion this is one of the best parts of the degree since you are able to implement your knowledge from lectures, and some of my fondest memories are working on practical tasks together with my friends in the lab. There is some group or pair work such as the group project (Part IB) and hardware labs (Part IA), however most of it is individual. For the majority of the practicals you are able to work in your own time and location, and upload your code for an online automated tester within a limited time frame. However, I still found it incredibly useful and fun to work with my friends to discuss problems and solutions together. The frequency of practicals depends on the courses in the timetable, and varies for each term.

Supervisions

The number of supervisions for each course greatly depends on the college. I had 4 supervisions a week in the first year, but in the second year the frequency has been less. It is very common to have weekend supervisions; however they require you to submit the work beforehand, which actually avoids you working in the weekend. A typical supervision is an hour-long class with two people and the supervisor. The supervisor will give you a set of questions to complete and submit beforehand. These will be marked and explained in the supervision. The supervision is also your chance to ask about any other parts of the course you don't understand, or anything further you want to discuss outside the scope of the lectures.

In our college, we have the freedom to schedule our own supervisions. This can allow flexibility if you are behind with a certain course, but you also have to be careful to manage your time well and structure your term. Other colleges may not have this system of booking supervisions, and a time for the class would be scheduled by the supervisor. If you are in a large college then you can expect your supervision partners to be from the same college, however for smaller colleges your partner may be from a different college.

Evening Time / Relaxation

It is really important to keep some time for socialising or relaxing in the week. You can join a club, attend formal dinners and college events, hang out in the games room etc. Whilst the workload may vary during the term, meaning there will probably be some nights spent in the library, there is time for fun as well. I find that having breaks like this often leads to more productive work overall.

Application Process

Personal Statement

In the personal statement they want to see passion for the subject. Since Computer Science A-Level is not compulsory, the interviewers would like you to demonstrate something you have done on your own to realise that Computer Science is a subject that you would like to study. This could include personal projects, learning to code via problem solving e.g. Project Euler questions, work experience, clubs inside or outside of school, hackathons or other coding competitions, courses (in person or online), contributing to open source projects, giving a technical presentation, participating in a computer related summer camp, reading relevant books etc. These are a few examples I could think of, but anything that involved you independently seeking out knowledge that sparked an interest in Computer Science would qualify. There is no compulsory level of technical knowledge that you need to apply, since the university knows everyone comes from different backgrounds. The colleges are also looking for a strong mathematical foundation so be sure to include anything that demonstrates good problem solving skills or shows your aptitude in Mathematics.

Admissions Assessment

All colleges will require you sit the CTMUA (also known as TMUA) admissions assessment before you are called for an interview. This is in the format of two multiple choice papers, the first one focusses on pure maths, and the second one contains more generic problem solving and logic type questions. There are a number of (C)TMUA papers available online for practice, however if you complete all of these the Oxford MAT paper would be good practice for extra material. Some colleges (named on Cambridge or individual college websites) additionally require you to sit the CSAT paper at interview. This has longer questions and requires written solutions. The focus here is on problem solving approaches and whether you can work through a complex problem. If you run out of CSAT practice material, then STEP questions are a good source of similar problems.

Interview

There are typically one or two half an hour interviews depending on the college. In these you will be asked one or two maths or problem-solving type questions, with the problem becoming harder and harder the more you progress through them. For this reason, don't expect to know everything at interview or to be able to answer everything fully - they will keep increasing the difficulty of the question in the time given. Throughout the interview it is important that you constantly think aloud and narrate why you are taking each step. This will help them understand how you are approaching the problem and help them guide you back on track if you go wrong. The problems can be deliberately vague so be sure to ask clarifying questions, and always attempt to offer up a solution or approach even though it might not be the best one. The interviewer will help you improve on it.

If you have multiple interviews then they might ask you about your personal statement, but this is again a chance for you to show your interest in the subject. There is no level of expected knowledge in Computer Science before you apply.

How is your Application Assessed?

Your Exam Performance

The Cambridge application process can feel very mysterious, but as we discussed in the first section of this book, there's nothing secret about it at all.

The first and most essential parts of your application are your GCSE and A Level grades. You might not think it needs mentioning, but hardly anyone applies to Cambridge, let alone gets in, with a collection of Bs and Cs. At the same time, the grades you'll need to achieve to secure your place once you've received an offer aren't a secret either. The standard offer for Computer Science is A*AA, including A level Mathematics and Further Maths. Most applicants have A levels in at least three science or mathematics subjects, and some Cambridge colleges actively require A level Physics.

So, you've got the grades. What next?

Your Reference

The next thing to consider is your reference. Ensuring that you have a great reference can be a huge help to your application, as it will give the admissions tutor a much clearer insight into what you are like as a student than your test results or your personal statement can. You should ask a teacher who knows you well, and with whom you have a good relationship, to write your reference if you can. Think of it as a review of you as a student, sent from one academic to another. You'd be much more likely to trust a restaurant review written by a professional chef if you were also a chef, so getting the right reference can be a crucial advantage to your application.

To help you and your referee – the teacher who writes the reference – make the most of it, we've provided a template and some key points at the back of this book. Your teacher will receive the same material, so you'll quite literally be on the same page when you come to discuss it.

Your Personal Statement

Finally, comes the Personal Statement. Over the past few years, as GCSE and A level grades have risen, the Personal Statement has become a less central part of the decision-making process for top universities. In practice, this means that if you haven't got the grades, there's a chance that they won't spend long assessing your statement. However, this means that the Personal Statements can be scrutinised far more closely.

A great Personal Statement can give the reader a window into the applicant's personality that takes them from being a name on a list to a prospective student that the reader is keen to meet. Think about it from the admissions tutor's perspective for a moment. They're trying to find not just the best prospective students, but the students that they're most interested in spending time with and teaching. In the Cambridge tutorial setting this is even more important – you might be spending hours and hours a week with a student, so making sure that you find them an engaging presence is a major factor.

Moreover, if you're applying for a subject that involves essay writing, you need to be able to demonstrate that you can actually write. Many applicants panic when faced with the new genre of Personal Statement and forget everything they once knew about good writing. A great personal statement will give the reader a hint of what an engaging, curious, and intelligent person you are. A truly great one will convey that message through clear, readable English prose. It's harder than you think, and while a personal statement alone won't get you an offer to study Computer Science at Cambridge, a dull, arrogant, or incurious one can easily ensure that you don't even get an interview.

Programme Timeline

The schedule laid out over the next few pages is a suggestion for how you might want to plan your studies over the course of the application process. It's not set in stone, but we've found that consistent efforts over a long period of time have a much more powerful impact than concentrated efforts if they are rushed.

If you find yourself falling behind on the Programme, identify the steps you need to catch up, discuss with your tutor the best way to respond and adapt your plan. For example, if you've only spent 20 of 30 hours with your tutor by the start of October, you'll need to schedule those hours quickly, so that you can get the full value out of them.

To help summarise things, we've also given you a set of milestones for how many hours of tuition, reading and prep you should complete on a month-by-month basis. This will help you to stay on track with the Programme, and to build your skills in a sustained way.

January

- Spend 1 hour with your tutor
- Read 1 book from the Reading List
- Complete Personal Statement content notes

February

- Complete 1 Mock Paper
- Spend 1 hour with your tutor
- Apply for work experience

March

- Complete 1 Mock Paper
- Spend 2 hours with your tutor
- Watch 10% of Online Academy
- Complete 10 practice questions a week

April

- Complete 1 Past Paper
- Spend 2 hours with your tutor
- Watch 10% of Online Academy
- Complete 10 practice questions a week
- Begin enrichment seminars
- Start the TMUA Guide

May

- Spend 3 hours with your tutor
- Watch 10% hours of the Online Academy
- Read 1 book from the Reading List
- Attend enrichment seminars
- Complete 10 practice questions a week
- Read Personal Statement Guide

June

- Complete 1 Past Paper
- Spend 3 hours with your tutor
- Watch 10% hours of Online Academy
- Attend enrichment seminars
- Complete 10 practice questions a week

July

- Complete 1 Past Paper
- Spend 3 hours with your tutor
- Finish reading 50% of the TMUA Guide
- Watch 15% of the Online Academy
- Attend enrichment seminars
- Read 1 book from the Reading List
- Personal Statement Course

August

- Complete 1 Past Paper
- Spend 3 hours with your tutor
- Finish reading 75% of the TMUA Guide
- Watch 15% of the Online Academy
- Attend enrichment seminars
- Complete work experience
- Complete first Personal Statement draft
- Complete 10 practice questions a week

September

- Personal Statement Course
- Re-sit 3 Mock Papers
- Spend 4 hours with your tutor
- Complete Personal Statement second draft
- Watch 15% of the Online Academy
- Read 1 book from the Reading List
- Attend enrichment seminars
- Complete 15 practice questions a week

October

- Intensive Admissions Test Course
- 1 mock interview
- Watch 15% of the Online Academy
- Spend 3 hours with your tutor
- Submit UCAS Application
- Re-sit all Past Papers

November

- Complete the Admissions Test
- Spend 4 hours with your tutor – 2 of those hours need to be mock interviews
- Read the Oxbridge Interview Guide
- Read 1 book from the Reading List
- Attend enrichment seminars
- Complete 1 mock interview with a friend
- Attend Interview Course

December

- Spend 1 hour with your tutor conducting a final mock interview
- Attend enrichment seminars
- Attend your Cambridge Interview

January

The beginning! 75% of our students who enrolled on a programme at this stage got their offers from Cambridge!

Key Tasks for this Month:

🎓 Pick where you're going to start on your Reading List, and make sure to finish your first book.

🎓 Personal Statement – make a list of all the things you could put into your personal statement: achievements, experiences, books, interests etc.

🎓 You'll go through this in depth with your tutor in your first session, exploring what is and is not worth putting into the Personal Statement and what admissions tutors are actually impressed by.

🎓 If you're torn between subject choices or between universities, now is also the time to be putting some research into it. There's no need to rush your decision, but the earlier it is made, the more you will be able to focus on the specific requirements of that course.

🎓 You'll have the option to have consultations with tutors from a range of subjects and universities. This will give you the opportunity to explore your options, find out what the courses will really involve (including differing chances of admission, what to expect at the other end of the degree etc), and make the most informed decision possible.

Key Reading for this Month

The Ultimate Oxbridge Collection (just the College Guide)

Your End of Month Goals: here you can write targets to meet, helping you stay on track.

1.

2.

3.

My Progress in January

Steps Forward Taken: What pieces of work have you completed, books read, or decisions made? Include clearly defined milestones to help you track your progress.

Reading Reflections: What new ideas, concepts, and problems did you encounter? How have they changed your thinking or opinions?

Efforts Committed: Take pride in the work you've done by keeping track of the hours you've put in.

Tutoring Sessions Completed:

Pages of Reading:

Past and Practice Papers Done:

Two Highs:

1.

2.

Two Lows:

1.

2.

On
Track

February

You've made a start, but you need to keep things ticking over. It's so easy to ignore deadlines that are far away, but consistent effort over long periods of time is a persistent marker of success.

Key Tasks for this Month:

🎓 Review your Personal Statement list – what is strong and what is missing? Start applying for work experience now. The good ones always go first!

🎓 You'll spend time with your expert tutors discussing what is going to make the biggest difference to your application, plus they will give guidance on what work experience opportunities to pursue and how to find them.

🎓 Sit your first timed mock A level paper and mark – this will give you a sense of where your weaknesses are and what you ought to be working on through the year.

🎓 You'll be able to go through the weak points with your tutor plus have full written feedback for essays.

Key Reading for this Month

The Ultimate UCAS Personal Statement Guide

Your End of Month Goals: here you can write targets to meet, helping you stay on track.

1.

2.

3.

My Progress in February

Steps Forward Taken: What pieces of work have you completed, books read, or decisions made? Include clearly defined milestones to help you to track your progress.

Reading Reflections: What new ideas, concepts, and problems did you encounter? How have they changed your thinking or opinions?

Efforts Committed: Take pride in the work you've done by keeping track of the hours you've put in.

Tutoring Sessions Completed:

Pages of Reading:

Past and Practice Papers Done:

Two Highs:

1.

2.

Two Lows:

1.

2.

On
Track

March

If you're considering giving something up for Lent, why not take something on instead? An hour of volunteering a week, some tutoring for younger years – there are lots of ways you could do more with your days, and now's a great time to start a good habit.

Key Tasks for this Month:

🎓 Subject and University ought to be decided by the end of March.

🎓 Same goes for work experience, a lot of the more impressive summer internships will likely be oversubscribed by now.

🎓 If you are one of our students and you do change your mind as to what subject or university you want to apply to, we will happily adjust resources and tutors to make sure you are getting the relevant support.

🎓 Start working on practice questions – you should be doing 10 questions a week from now until test day.

🎓 Complete another mock TMUA and mark it, to go through with your tutor.

🎓 Start watching the Online Academy videos - start at the very beginning with the Syllabus Walkthrough.

🎓 Our students have a guided syllabus to take them through everything that needs to be covered this year and how to break it up into manageable chunks.

Key Reading for this Month

One book from the reading list

Your End of Month Goals: here you can write targets to meet, helping you stay on track.

1.

2.

3.

My Progress in March

Steps Forward Taken: What pieces of work have you completed, books read, or decisions made? Include clearly defined milestones to help you to track your progress.

Reading Reflections: What new ideas, concepts, and problems did you encounter? How have they changed your thinking or opinions?

Efforts Committed: Take pride in the work you've done by keeping track of the hours you've put in.

Tutoring Sessions Completed:

Pages of Reading:

Past and Practice Papers Done:

Two Highs:

1.

2.

And Two Lows:

1.

2.

On Track

April

Start dedicating more time to your mocks and less time to the admissions process. The predicted grades are an important aspect that the admissions tutors consider, and they will depend vastly on these mocks. An hour a week total will be enough to fit around revision.

If you need any subject specific guidance – use your tutors! They are the most valuable resource you have and will likely have sat the exams you are sitting. If you're struggling, they will be able to help.

To help balance out your preparation, the **UniAdmissions Enrichment Seminars** start this month. You can read more about these later in the book.

Key Tasks for this Month

- Give yourself some respite in between revision.
- Attend your first Enrichment Seminar – this should help you develop the academic tools to start using your reading to support your application, and your intellectual development as a whole.
- Keep up with practising questions each day - you should be building a habit of 10 questions a week.
- Continue watching the Online Academy - a little each day - making sure you make notes in any area you are weak in or need a little help in understanding, so you can cover it with your tutor.

Key Reading for this Month

One book from your reading list

Your End of Month Goals: here you can write targets to meet, helping you stay on track.

1.

2.

3.

My Progress in April

Steps Forward Taken: What pieces of work have you completed, books read, or decisions made? Include clearly defined milestones to help you to track your progress.

Reading Reflections: What new ideas, concepts, and problems did you encounter? How have they changed your thinking or opinions?

Efforts Committed: Take pride in the work you've done by keeping track of the hours you've put in.

Tutoring Sessions Completed:

Pages of Reading:

Past and Practice Papers Done:

Two Highs:

1.

2.

And Two Lows:

1.

2.

On
Track

May

Mocks!! Good luck with them!

But once they're done, onto the next challenge! Refresh yourself on the admissions process and where your application needs the most work. Start working on that – at least 2 hours a week.

Key Tasks for this Month:

🎓 Get back on track with your UCAS application.

🎓 Keep on track with the Enrichment Seminars. If you miss a few, be sure to catch up with the recordings afterwards.

🎓 You'll know from your regular reports if you're falling behind. You've still got time to recover and succeed, and your tutor will know exactly what needs to be done over the summer to catch up.

🎓 Pick another book from the reading list that you've been itching to get into.

🎓 Don't abandon the Online Academy either!

Key Reading for this Month

The Ultimate Oxbridge Collection (Personal Statement Guide)

Your End of Month Goals: here you can write targets to meet, helping you stay on track.

1.

2.

3.

My Progress in May

Steps Forward Taken: What pieces of work have you completed, books read, or decisions made? Include clearly defined milestones to help you to track your progress.

Reading Reflections: What new ideas, concepts, and problems did you encounter? How have they changed your thinking or opinions?

Efforts Committed: Take pride in the work you've done by keeping track of the hours you've put in.

Tutoring Sessions Completed:

Pages of Reading:

Past and Practice Papers Done:

Two Highs:

1.

2.

And Two Lows:

1.

2.

On
Track

June

Summer time! It's getting warm outside, and you'll have more free time as the end of term approaches, but stay motivated and use this time constructively. All our textbooks come as e-books too, so you can take the learning with you even if you're travelling.

Key Tasks for this Month:

🎓 Keep up with the Enrichment Seminars. These are still **90** minutes a week but spend time on the admissions test too!

🎓 You'll be directed by your tutors as to how best to be spending your time – no point spending your time on something unless it's going to directly improve your application!

🎓 You should have completed the Personal Statement section of the Oxbridge Collection textbook by now.

🎓 You will also be in full swing with the enrichment seminars; make sure to follow up ones you found particularly interesting with further research, discussion and reading – especially if they are topics you can add to your personal statement.

🎓 Complete a past paper and mark it to go through with your tutor.

Key Reading for this Month

One book from your reading list

Your End of Month Goals: here you can write targets to meet, helping you stay on track.

1.

2.

3.

My Progress in June

Steps Forward Taken: What pieces of work have you completed, books read, or decisions made? Clearly defined milestones to help you to track your progress.

Reading Reflections: What new ideas, concepts, and problems did you encounter? How have they changed your thinking or opinions?

Efforts Committed: Take pride in the work you've done by keeping track of the hours you've put in.

Tutoring Sessions Completed:

Pages of Reading:

Past and Practice Papers Done:

Two Highs:

1.

2.

And Two Lows:

1.

2.

On
Track

July

Open days! Go and see your chosen university (COVID-19 permitting). This will really help you with choosing your college. You wouldn't buy a pair of shoes without trying them on first, so make sure to take your time and make a well-informed choice.

Events this Month

UniAdmissions Personal Statement Intensive Day Course

Key Tasks for this Month:

- Get the first draft of your Personal Statement marked. By now you should know what to put in it, so the focus is on how best to phrase it and fit it all into the line limit.
- We mark as many personal statement drafts as a student sends to us. From now on send at least one draft a month to be marked.
- You should also be spending a couple of hours a week going through tricky interview questions.
- You'll have 1:1 tutorials to go over interview techniques and tips, as well as going through specific Cambridge-style questions.
- If you haven't already, start watching the Online Academy videos, and aim to watch 25% of them by the end of this month.
- Pick another book from the reading list – you may find one or two of them useful for your upcoming enrichment seminars!

Key Reading for this Month

One book from the reading list.

Your End of Month Goals: here you can write targets to meet, helping you stay on track.

1.

2.

3.

My Progress in July

Steps Forward Taken: What pieces of work have you completed, books read, or decisions made? Include clearly defined milestones to help you to track your progress.

Reading Reflections: What new ideas, concepts, and problems did you encounter? How they changed your thinking or opinions?

Efforts Committed: Take pride in the work you've done by keeping track of the hours you've put in.

Tutoring Sessions Completed:

Pages of Reading:

Past and Practice Papers Done:

Two Highs:

1.

2.

And Two Lows:

1.

2.

On
Track

August

Long sunny summer days aren't particularly conducive to hard work –
we know. Enjoy the weather and see your friends (COVID-19
permitting), but make sure you're still allocating time each week to your
application; even in weeks when you're on work experience, a 20-
minute commute can be much more useful if you spend it reading.

Key Tasks for this Month:

🎓 Finish your first Personal Statement draft.

🎓 Work experience! In total, you ought to be spending around a
month on work experience. This can be made up of multiple
different placements, which can be particularly helpful if you're
unsure about your degree and need more context for what you
might do with it.

🎓 Keep up with your reading and check in with your tutor on your
personal statement; see if you can begin refining it.

Key Reading for this Month

One book from the reading list

Your End of Month Goals: here you can write targets to meet,
helping you stay on track.

1.

2.

3.

My Progress in August

Steps Forward Taken: What pieces of work have you completed, books read, or decisions made? Include clearly defined milestones to help you to track your progress.

Reading Reflections: What new ideas, concepts, and problems did you encounter? How have they changed your thinking or opinions?

Efforts Committed: Take pride in the work you've done by keeping track of the hours you've put in.

Tutoring Sessions Completed:

Pages of Reading:

Past and Practice Papers Done:

Two Highs:

1.

2.

And Two Lows:

1.

2.

On
Track

Early September

This is where things get serious! We've split September and October into smaller chunks for this guide, so you can really target your preparation in these final key weeks. Remember, some applicants will only just be starting now, so keep up the pace to stay ahead of the pack.

Events this Month

UniAdmissions Personal Statement Intensive Course

Key Tasks for this Month:

🎓 You'll be back from holidays, but you still need to be putting time into your application. Just because you've got a head start on lots of other people doesn't mean you should get complacent.

🎓 Grab another book from the reading list.

🎓 Make sure to incorporate any experiences, work or discoveries from over the holidays into your personal statement. Showing that your passion for the subject comes from relevant experience is much, much more convincing than just saying it. This will give you your second personal statement draft.

Key Reading for this Month

The Ultimate Cambridge Interview Guide (Computer Science, Maths, Physics, Engineering)

Your End of Month Goals: here you can write targets to meet, helping you stay on track.

1.

2.

3.

My Progress in Early September

Steps Forward Taken: What pieces of work have you completed, books read, or decisions made? Include clearly defined milestones to help you to track your progress.

Reading Reflections: What new ideas, concepts, and problems did you encounter? How have they changed your thinking or opinions?

Efforts Committed: Take pride in the work you've done by keeping track of the hours you've put in.

Tutoring Sessions Completed:

Pages of Reading:

Past and Practice Papers Done:

Two Highs:

1.

2.

And Two Lows:

1.

2.

On Track

Mid-September

It's only a month until the application deadline, so make sure you're planning out your time intelligently. If you need to spend longer on your Personal Statement, make sure to give it the time it deserves without neglecting the rest of your preparation.

Key Tasks for this Month:

🎓 Give your Personal Statement the time it needs, and don't be afraid to ask for more support from tutors, or to rethink what you're doing with it. You've still got a month, and now is the best time to rewrite or restructure if that's what you think it going to work best for your application.

My Progress in Mid-September

Steps Forward Taken: What pieces of work have you completed, books read, or decisions made? Include clearly defined milestones to help you to track your progress.

Reading Reflections: What new ideas, concepts, and problems did you encounter? How have they changed your thinking or opinions?

Efforts Committed: Take pride in the work you've done by keeping track of the hours you've put in.

Tutoring Sessions Completed:

Pages of Reading:

Past and Practice Papers Done:

Two Highs:

1.

2.

And Two Lows:

1.

2.

On
Track

Late September

Not long to go now! You should be seeing the benefits of having a head start over your peers; feeling relaxed, confident, and full of good ideas about Personal Statements to share.

Key Tasks for this Month:

🎓 This is a great time to back over any sessions or key concepts you're struggling with, and don't be afraid to reach out to your tutor, or Programme Manager for support.

🎓 Write a new draft of your Personal Statement and arrange another practice interview.

My Progress in Late September

Steps Forward Taken: What pieces of work have you completed, books read, or decisions made? Include clearly defined milestones to help you to track your progress.

Reading Reflections: What new ideas, concepts, and problems did you encounter? How have they changed your thinking or opinions?

Efforts Committed: Take pride in the work you've done by keeping track of the hours you've put in.

Tutoring Sessions Completed:

Pages of Reading:

Past and Practice Papers Done:

Two Highs:

1.

2.

And Two Lows:

1.

2.

On
Track

Early October

You want to spend your time here focusing on final tweaks to your Personal Statement and maximising your portfolio of experience.

Key Tasks for this Month:

- This is a great time for a Mock Interview. Make sure to take time to reflect on the feedback and plan for your next one.
- Again, take your feedback to your personal tutor as soon as possible. They'll be able to make sure you are polishing things off well.
- Final improvements on your Personal Statement. It'll be too late after the deadline, so don't miss anything!
- Fill out UCAS application form! Some people like to fill out the form on Day One; but whatever you do, don't get into a panic filling out your GCSEs at the last minute!

Key Reading for this Month

The Ultimate Cambridge Interview Guide (Computer Science, Maths, Physics, Engineering)

Your End of Month Goals: here you can write targets to meet, helping you stay on track.

1.

2.

3.

My Progress in Early October

Steps Forward Taken: What pieces of work have you completed, books read, or decisions made? Include clearly defined milestones to help you to track your progress.

Reading Reflections: What new ideas, concepts, and problems did you encounter? How have they changed your thinking or opinions?

Efforts Committed: Take pride in the work you've done by keeping track of the hours you've put in.

Tutoring Sessions Completed:

Pages of Reading:

Past and Practice Papers Done:

Two Highs:

1.

2.

And Two Lows:

1.

2.

On
Track

Late October

UCAS? Check. Interview? Coming right up. You've spent months preparing for this, if you've followed this guide so far, you should be more than ready, and find it easier than you expected on the day.

Key Tasks for this Month:

🎓 Finish reading the *Oxbridge Interview Guide*. It'll give you a sense of what's to come, and help you plan your interview sessions with your tutor.

🎓 If you've mentioned any books in your Personal Statement that you haven't actually read, start them now. More people do this than you'd think, and it's an easy mistake to make, so be smart and plan your time accordingly.

My Progress in Late October

Steps Forward Taken: What pieces of work have you completed, books read, or decisions made? Include clearly defined milestones to help you to track your progress.

Reading Reflections: What new ideas, concepts, and problems did you encounter? How have they changed your thinking or opinions?

Efforts Committed: Take pride in the work you've done by keeping track of the hours you've put in.

Tutoring Sessions Completed:

Pages of Reading:

Past and Practice Papers Done:

Two Highs:

1.

2.

And Two Lows:

1.

2.

On
Track

November

You'll hear back this month, normally during the last week, whether you've been invited for interview or not. If you haven't heard by the end of November, don't be afraid to call the college and check – they have been known to forget!

Events this Month

UniAdmissions Interviews Intensive Day course

Key Tasks for this Month:

🎓 Do your second and third Mock Interview – you mustn't forget about this. The admissions tests are important, but the interview will be right around the corner.

🎓 Use the rest of your time going through the feedback on those mocks, and maybe test out new skills you've learnt from the feedback by asking a friend or family member to interview you too.

🎓 Keep up you reading: grab another book from the reading list, or start to study recent research papers and topical subjects. If you've done nothing since the Personal Statement was submitted, interviewers may doubt your interest in the subject is genuine.

🎓 If you're stuck for reading, ask your tutor for tips – now is a good time to read some fiction if you've been focusing on non-fiction in your reading, or vice versa.

Key Reading for this Month

One book from the reading list

Your End of Month Goals: here you can write targets to meet, helping you stay on track.

1.

2.

3.

My Progress in November

Steps Forward Taken: What pieces of work have you completed, books read, or decisions made? Include clearly defined milestones to help you to track your progress.

Reading Reflections: What new ideas, concepts, and problems did you encounter? How have they changed your thinking or opinions?

Efforts Committed: Take pride in the work you've done by keeping track of the hours you've put in.

Tutoring Sessions Completed:

Pages of Reading:

Two Highs:

1.

2.

Two Lows:

1.

2.

On
Track

December

It's interview time! Make sure you're well rested, and above all enjoy the opportunity to stay at an incredible Cambridge college (or see one through a webcam)! We'll be here to support you up to the interview – any last-minute questions, send them our way!

Events this Month

Your Cambridge interviews.

Key Tasks for this Month

🎓 Conduct one final interview with your tutor, just for some final feedback.

🎓 Relax, get a good night's sleep, and do yourself justice. You've worked hard to get this far, so make sure that you're not left with regrets.

🎓 Relax after your interview but be sure to prepare in good time for the next one you may have.

🎓 The final enrichment sessions complete at the start of the month.

Your End of Month Goals: here you can write targets to meet, helping you stay on track.

1.

2.

3.

Student Honour Code

I agree to:

- Pro-actively schedule all of my tutoring sessions in advance with my tutor.
- Respond to all emails from my tutors and tuition manager within 48 hours.
- Return any calls from my tutors and tuition manager within 24 hours.
- Attend every scheduled session as planned and on time.
- Give my tutor at least 24 hours notice if I need to cancel/reschedule a tuition session.
- Complete all homework in a timely manner and return to tutor at least 2 days before the next scheduled session.
- Prepare any questions prior to the scheduled session.
- Complete all the mock papers and past papers as per the schedule.

Name:

Signature:

Date:

Your Programme

	Materials	Hours of Work
Intensive Courses	Intensive Interview Course	7
	Intensive Personal Statement Course	7
	Intensive TMUA Course	7
Groundwork	Work Experience Outreach	4
	Recommended Reading x3 Books	30
	Personal Statement Writing & Revisions	8
	UCAS Reference Guidance	4
Fundamentals	Interview Preparation	10
	TMUA Past Papers x 5	18
	Exam Success Academy	8
	TMUA Academy	10
Textbooks	Ultimate Oxbridge Interview Guide	4
	Ultimate TMUA Guide	24
	Ultimate UCAS Personal Statement Guide	3
Tutor Contact	1-to-1 Tuition	30
	Tuition Prep/Homework	30
	Weekly Enrichment Supervisions	30
	Total	**234**

Guided Study

You will have hours of online lectures, practice questions, further reading and specimen papers. You are a smart student who revels in independent learning and discovery. These are not the kind of things you need a tutor for, but they are crucial for you to develop your understanding.

'Little and often' is one of the most important mantras for any academic. Spread evenly over the year, the work will be far more manageable; but in addition, principles of learning dictate that the skills and knowledge you are working on will not only be better established, but they will stay with you for far longer in life too. The guided study won't just get you through these challenges; it will give you the skills and academic rigour to succeed in the future.

It is a common pitfall to practice the things you find easy and to put off the things you find hard – your tutors will be able to help you identify what's holding you back, but it's up to you to commit to improving those areas.

In terms of further reading and subject enrichment, you shouldn't be researching things further because you have to; you should be doing it because it is interesting! You won't be interested in all topics you come across, which is why starting broad with your reading lists is vital; you can then zoom in on topics that you personally enjoy.

Enrichment Seminars

Our enrichment seminars are the secret sauce of your application; broadening your horizons and deepening your engagement with ideas in ways that will benefit your interview and personal statement.

Over thirty-five sessions, you'll explore a range of topics in medical and scientific fields, giving you the tools and context to understand the subject broadly enough to impress at interview. These sessions represent a full term's worth of ideas, so don't be intimidated by the breadth of what you'll be discussing!

If there are topics which catch your interest and you wish to explore further, it's always worth mentioning this to your personal tutor so that you can develop your understanding individually, with a focus on how that links to your other interests, experience and skills.

If you have questions about the content of a seminar which you'd like the lead tutor to answer, you can submit them to your supervision lead via email, or in the chat, and they'll reply individually; or address the question at the beginning of the next session.

The email address for submission of questions is tutors@uniadmissions.co.uk - just make sure to put your supervision stream ('Computer Science') in the subject line of the email.

STEM Enrichment Seminars

1. Lessons from the History of Science

Scientists and mathematicians are often (surprisingly) reluctant to examine how science as we know it today developed. In some cases, this is based on an unwillingness to face uncomfortable and unethical truths. However, in the majority of cases, it is based on the assumption that how we do it now is the best it has been done so far, and is therefore the only springboard for innovation required. Often, this could not be further from the truth. In this session, students will be briefly introduced to the history of science via a number of examples, as well as applying theory from a variety of disciplines with a view to developing their understanding of how science works, why science works, and their role in understanding the world around them.

2. The Fine Line: 'Economics vs Science'

This session will focus on the degree of conflict between economists and scientists in top organisations through time. Students will evaluate whether either is indebted to the other. Do poor economic conditions cultivate the best scientific breakthroughs or do these occur at times of great prosperity? Students will gain a wider appreciation of how the two subjects are intertwined as well as some of the economic barriers facing the scientific community.

3. Mathematical Modelling

Can you really model the spread of COVID-19? Is weather forecasting the best mathematical model in society? In this session, students will learn about mathematical models; what they are, what they are based on and how to create one. Alongside case studies, students will examine the impact mathematical modelling has on our day to day lives. Additionally, they will consider whether human dependency on these models will only increase, and propose their own mathematical models to help solve current problems.

4. Game Theory

Split or Steal? Would your partner in crime really stick to Game Theory? Are Tobacco companies better off without advertising? Game Theory brings with it a fascination and applicability to real-world scenarios that have produced some memorable moments. Students will have the opportunity to explore and discuss a number of case studies. The effects of rational and irrational decision makers will be examined as well as how they may have already exacted game theory in their day to day lives.

5. Philosophy and Logic

This session will cover a range of Philosophical frameworks within which scientists can work, taking a look at current world philosophical ideas which scientists should work on. We will then switch to logical frameworks to convert world problems into solvable problems.

6. Maths: The Language of Nature

This session will ask students to consider whether maths is a fundamental part of the natural world, or a human construct – with all the constraints that brings. They will look at times when mathematical theory and observation haven't lined up – and discuss whether the ever-increasing complexity of maths is a hint that a simpler 'unified' theory is going to rewrite the rule book, or whether it is an inevitability when describing an infinitely complex universe.

7. Probability and Perception

This session will examine probability and how it is perceived by society, as well as some of the paradoxes that probability leads to. Just how likely are you to win the lottery? Why did one game show cause such dispute? Students will work through a number of case studies that demonstrate just how important probability is, discuss whether society truly knows what odds they are faced with, and find out just how likely sharing a birthday with someone in their class really is.

8. 'Big Data' & The Art (or science?) of Predictions

This session will take an in-depth look at the field of data science: what it is, how it has developed, ethical issues, and areas of interest for the future. Students will then discuss the more social aspects of data science: how to make predictions, the importance of good predictions and the risks to society of failing to foresee the inevitable.

9. Blockchain and its applications

This session will cover the general aspect of finance and how cryptography is changing the system. We will move on to the details of blockchain and how it being implemented into the world as well as the impact Non-Fungible Tokens have. Ethereum's smart contracts can also be looked at.

10. Scientific Creativity

This session will explore both the science of creativity, and the value of creativity in science. Mathematicians, scientists and engineers are often keen to point out the value of creativity to their disciplines, in an attempt to overcome stereotypes about both the people and the thought processes which make up 'science'. But can this value be quantified? Is scientific creativity unique, or just another facet of the innovation which underpins the arts? And do people in scientific fields actually 'walk the walk' when it comes to innovation, or fall into the human trap of guarding against change?

11. Why Challenging Assumptions is the Key to Good Science

Is the Big Bang really where it all began? Challenging assumptions has led to the progression of science. In this session we will look at some key case studies that led to the development of important scientific material and theories today. More importantly, the session will encourage and develop the student's own analytical mindset, allowing them to begin to challenge assumptions themselves, an important tool for any successful scientist to have.

12. Designed for Failure

This session focuses mainly on technical failure, particularly the failure of products and concepts relating to STEM. Failure is a vital component of the scientific process and remains so when this bleeds into product design. In this session, we will look at the connection in the modern world between failure and negativity, and whether this can be at least partially undone. We will also look at ways to ensure that failure, when it does happen, is manageable and safe, and as a part of this we will also take a look at planned obsolescence.

13. Technological Development

This session will seek to define 'technology' - in some fields this will be relatively straightforward, but in others it will be less clear. Students will be led through a range of case studies to explore the key factors underpinning a range of technological developments in the 20th and 21st century, and will then look at how these can be applied (on a smaller scale) to the work they seek to develop at university and beyond.

14. Nuclear: Future or Fading?

Students will be encouraged to examine the ever-increasing energy demands of a growing population and what place nuclear power may have over the next 30 years. Case studies will focus on the best and worst of nuclear power through time, and how politicians attempt to shroud the science from the public. Is it ethical to promise nuclear safety? Is it immoral to sensationalise its risk? Students will be encouraged to formulate their own opinions and ethical standpoints through debate and discussion.

15. Artificial Intelligence: Pandora's Box?

The rise of the machines or human ingenuity? Through a number of case studies, students will assess the potential effects of Artificial Intelligence on our lives moving forwards, and what it spells for a number of job sectors. The greatest invention or an untimely demise? Only time and this session will tell.

16. TBC

17. Is Reality Real?

Are you really reading this? Is the infamous double slit experiment the big clue? This session will look at a number of case studies that argue for and against our entire existence being a simulation. Students will improve their ability to discuss abstract topics and learn how to propose their own evidence in support of or against theories. This topic is a fantastic way to examine both philosophical and scientific reasoning, and how the two can support and conflict with each other.

18. The Evolution of Consciousness

In this session students will work towards how they believe consciousness should be defined, how it developed and whether all living creatures have the evolutional ability to reach a sentient state. They will examine questions such as: did consciousness just turn on? Are humans the only living organism to be conscious? What parameters define it?

19. Computers

80 years ago, a 'computer' only existed in the papers of distinguished mathematicians, and even as recently as 50 years ago it was not uncommon to have a computer the same size as a room. This seminar will look at the extremely rapid development of computers, compared to most other technologies being used, and the implication of this. Students will then go on to hypothesise as to what a world would be like if key technologies involved in computer production had never been created.

20. 2050 – Is It Possible?

UK law states "the net UK carbon account for the year 2050 [must be] at least 100% lower than the 1990 baseline". This ambitious target will require dramatic changes to our lives and the embracing of new emerging technologies. In this seminar students will look at how this target could be met; looking at how realistic it is that enough scientific breakthrough will occu, or if it will be necessary for us to face a major change to our lifestyles.

21. Science Vs Misinformation

The headline "A new study has shown [x]" is a familiar sight in the news media. However, often when you probe deeper into these stories the claims can be dubious at best! Students will look at how statistical cherry picking can cause almost anything to be shown to be true, and how science is trying to combat this effect. In a world increasing being described as 'Post truth', how can science remain true to its roots of proof and evidence?

22. TBC

23. Biology, The Future of Physics

From data storage to humanoid robots, we are increasingly gaining inspiration for our engineering exploits from the natural world. In this seminar students will identify areas of biology that are increasingly inspiring engineering and physics research in seemingly disconnected areas. For example, the human brain remains the most powerful computer on the planet – how can we harness this in the world of regular computing? Is it inevitable that eventually engineering will have more of a synergy with biology rather than physics?

24. COVID-19 – Lessons Learned

With the pandemic (hopefully) in the rear-view mirror, it is only correct that we look back and reflect on the implications it has for the wider world of science. Students will look at how the scientific method was adapted in the face of difficult circumstances and how – in record time – rigorous science came to the rescue. The seminar will then also look at how scientific communication should (or shouldn't) change as a result – would you be in favour of a weekly press conference by scientific experts looking at the latest scientific issues of the day?

25. TBC

26. Entrepreneurs: The Strengths and Weaknesses of Scientific Innovators

 Many students may be thinking about starting their own business or developing their own products during or after their degree. This session will start by examining a series of case studies, both past and present, which students can learn from. The session will end with some information on business theory in start-ups, for students who wish to learn more.

27. Changing the Way We Think

Has the way humans think changed over the past century? Is Generation Alpha set to have the biggest cognitive differences? Throughout this session, the way in which humans learn and think will be critically analysed, covering key topics such as neural plasticity and the mechanism of cognitive development. We will debate influences on the cognitive skills of Generation Alpha and what this means for societies moving forward. Key Case studies will also pose arguments for and against our ability to change the way we think with increasing time. Students will begin to appreciate and understand how they can change/develop their own scientific mindset and the way in which they think.

28. Risk – How to Determine Good Risk?

Risk is at the forefront of everything we do: when to cross the road, buy or sell a stock, or change jobs. Are the ways in which we calculate and perceive risk different? This session will compare human 'gut instinct' and the mathematical techniques that calculate good and bad risk. Is the gut the best at risk determination after all?

29. The Meaning of 'Profession'

An important, and often overlooked, part of any admissions process is the need for students to demonstrate their aims and objectives long-term. This session will start by looking at techniques for developing long-term plans, as well as the importance of flexibility in any planning. In doing this, students will be prompted to think about their chosen profession – do we hold engineers to the same standards as we hold doctors? What does it mean to be a 'scientist' or 'mathematician'?

30. Science in Society: The Art of Scientific Communication

Students will discuss what place scientists have in our society; their importance as well as how they are received. Analysis, in the form of discussion, will explore the variety of different ways and levels science is communicated across society. Whilst not everyone will understand science on the same level, is it important that society at large has some understanding? This session will help students in their ability to understand complex material and deliver it to audiences of varying scientific ability in an accessible way – an important skill for a scientist to possess.

31. TBC

32. Sustainability

This session will explore current topical issues surrounding the theme of environment, development, and sustainability. Students should begin by asking themselves how they would define 'sustainable' - and whether there can ever be a usable, universal definition.

33. Thinking Scientifically: Nature vs Nurture

The age-old question: could you be smarter? Students will have the opportunity to discuss and debate their opinions alongside study of a number of case studies that discuss the issue at length. Students will also get the opportunity to evaluate how intelligence can be measured and whether it is defined unilaterally across the world.

34. Scientific Ethics

"Your scientists were so preoccupied with whether or not they could, they didn't stop to think about if they should" is a succinct summary (from the Jurassic Park films!) of a key scientific issue. This session will cover a range of ethical frameworks within which scientists work, including a series of case studies which demonstrate possible difficulties with scientific ethics, as well as leading students to create a personal understanding of what they mean when they say we 'should' do something.

35. Have We Gone Too Far? A Battle of Morality

This session will focus on defining morality and its place in science and society; just how moral is science currently? Students will be encouraged to debate whether morality can both create and solve problems in society. Controversial case studies will be presented and students will be encouraged to weigh up both morality and immorality, from a scientific aspect, in their ability to create or solve issues.

36. Free Session

This session will provide the opportunity to look over the content of previous sessions and consider how, over the course of the programme, the student's perceptions, ideology and outlook may have changed. The second half of the session will focus on encouraging students to present an ideology or statement to the group and engaging in scientific and ethical debate.

37. TBC

38. TBC

39. Why STEM?

Science and engineering; STM; STEM; STEMM (Science, Technology, Engineering, Maths & Medicine). This grouping of subjects has gone through many incarnations; are they all the same or are there differences? In this seminar students will look at all of these subjects and how they should (or should not) be grouped. Is there any reason other subjects, such as geography or psychology, aren't included in this grouping; what is so special about these 4 (or five) subjects?

40. Teaching STEM

It is often said, "If you really want to master something, teach it." In this seminar, students will examine how each of the different STEM subjects is taught, all the way from pre-exam years to undergraduate level. Is there any one 'best' way to teach STEM and is it the same for the different subjects? Should we teach school science in the same way that undergraduates are taught? The seminar will finish with discussion around what changes should be made to STEM teaching and how they could be implemented.

41. Science to Engineering

Science and engineering are often described as a spectrum, with science being theoretical and engineering being the more practical side of the same subject. This seminar will examine how true this observation is; looking at areas where science and engineering cross over and areas in which they diverge. Students will then examine where other subjects fall on this spectrum, such as mathematics and humanities, and try to establish a way of mapping all these subjects onto one simple diagram.

42. Science in The Real World

Often engineering is seen as a practical subject whereas science is seen as a much more theoretical endeavour. This seminar will endeavour to show students where pure science can be seen and appreciated in the real world, but will also consider whether it is possible to ever have science without engineering. The seminar will then go on to peel back another layer and try to see whether any pure mathematical concepts can be seen in the 'real world'.

43. The Great Problems

Despite great advances in technology, many great unsolved problems remain. In this seminar students will be introduced to a broad range of (as yet) unsolved problems in the world of science, technology and mathematics; including some of the 'Millennium Prize Problems' which carry a hefty reward for their solution. Will these problems ever be solved and how important is it that we continue to seek questions to which we so far have no solution?

44. TBC
45. TBC

Intensive Courses

As part of your programme, you've reserved a place on exclusive intensive day or weekend courses. All courses are taught by our Cambridge tutors, so you know you can focus on the areas which really make the difference to Cambridge admissions tutors in particular.

All of these courses allow you to make rapid progress on an individual aspect of your application, over a day or a weekend in London. They're also all pre-recorded as part of our online academy, so you can go back and revisit any areas you're particularly unsure of in your own time, to make sure everything sticks!

Full logistical details of your courses (when and where) are included in your programme folder, which you will have been emailed when you joined the programme. We'll also send you a reminder email the week before each course.

They will also give you a chance to meet the UniAdmissions team face to face and to meet fellow Cambridge applicants. If you've been worrying about the interview, meeting people who are in the same boat can be really helpful and is a great chance to make friends and socialise at this hectic time.

If you have any questions about your courses, you're always welcome to contact your Tuition Manager, or our Courses Manager (at info@uniadmissions.co.uk).

We also like to use these courses as a chance to meet parents and teachers, so if they'd like to have a chat with us face to face, they're welcome to join us for a coffee for the first hour after the course start time, or for the last hour of the course. We'll be more than happy to answer any questions about the process, and we're always delighted to put faces to names when we get the chance, so we hope you'll find the time to say hello in person at one of the day courses!

The courses included in your programme are:

The Personal Statement Course

This course will take you through the information and writing style you need to craft a stand-out Personal Statement. You'll go from ideas to a complete first draft over the course of the day, allowing you to target your independent study time and tutor consultations much more effectively.

It's good to arrive with some ideas of the activities and skills you want to mention, but you don't need to bring a complete personal statement!

Prepare for the course: by making sure you bring a pad of paper, pens, sticky notes, water, some snacks and some initial ideas jotted down for your Personal Statement. Make sure you have plenty of rest the night before the course as it is a full day.

The Interview Course

This course packs performance coaching and interview techniques, subject-specific tutorials, and 2 Cambridge mock interviews into a weekend!

The practice you've done for your admissions test will often give you a massive head-start with practising questions of the difficulty (if not the style) that you can expect in your interview.

The key to success in your Cambridge interview is keeping your calm, knowing the material, and being able to justify your thoughts and logic - you'll practice all of these, and have the opportunity to ask questions to a range of Cambridge students and graduates in this intensive course.

Prepare for the course: by making sure you bring a pad of paper, pens, sticky notes, water and some snacks. Some students like to dress in the outfit they may wear to their actual interview to help get them into the right frame of mind - others wear comfortable clothing to help them relax - it's entirely up to you, but do consider both options. Make sure you have read as much of your reading list as possible, and that you are up to date on all subject-relevant current affairs. Make sure you have plenty of rest the night before the course as it is two full days.

Online Academy

What is the Online Academy?

The Online Academy is a series of online videos where you can learn about the techniques required for great A-level grades. These are prepared by our top tutors, and will give you an outstanding grounding in what you need to know before you sit your mocks.

The Academy consists of short tutorials on all the aspects of the test syllabus, ensuring that you'll have a complete understanding of the range of material you'll need to engage with.

Each video has a comprehensive revision of the subject to give you a deep understanding of the material. Each section includes at least one sample question and fully worked solution, which you can refer to during your revision.

The aim of the Online Academy is for you to be able to answer all the easy questions in your own time, freeing up your one-to-one tuition time for more detailed and fine-grained work.

Personal Tuition

There are some things you cannot work out intuitively; some things that you need to be taught, no matter how talented you may be. Personal tuition covers the classroom aspect of preparation; except that, instead of one teacher spread thinly across many students, this tutor is dedicated to working with you through your particular problem areas.

They aren't going to hold your hand. They are going to push you, and help you develop into an independent thinker. Consider them your personal mentor for how to be the ideal Cambridge candidate. They know how it's done; they were one themselves! They'll develop a plan for you, and they have the knowhow to help you stick to it. You just need to be committed, keen to learn and ready to dedicate time to achieving your goals.

Your tutors will initially want to assess you and your application, to identify the key areas for development throughout the year. Your tutorials will be structured to target each of these areas, develop it into a strength, and move on to the next weakness.

Like a real Cambridge lecture, tutorial or supervision, you mustn't show up empty handed. The tutor will expect you to have been doing your own research and groundwork so that the time you spend with them is focused on development and enrichment. They aren't here to learn the syllabus for you; they're here to help you become the best student you can be. Come with ideas; come with discussions and questions in mind so that your time with your tutor is put to best use.

The harder you work in your own time, the more you will get out of these tutorials and the stronger you will be as a candidate. It's as simple as that! Tutors are there to give guidance on anything to do with your application, so use their expertise! Yes, you may be planning on working on your Personal Statement in one session; but if you are anxious about College choice or the UCAS form, then bring it up and they will be able to guide you accordingly. These sessions will be like a real Cambridge tutorial, so if a topic has come up and spiralled into a debate… that isn't you getting off topic, that is academia! The ability to delve into a subject and explore it in depth is exactly what the admissions tutors will be looking for.

Top Tips from Your Tutors

Things I wish I had known before I applied:

-   Read as broadly as possible – it will help with your application, your studies once you get in, and also may lead you to decide another course is more appropriate for you.
-   Pick a city you would like to live in for 3 years or more - make sure to visit it if you can!
-   Look for people who inspire you to do something similar and see if they are attached to any university departments.
-   Think about the practical skills and experiences you can gain from your degree and what will be interesting and useful after university.
-   Choosing the right course is a big decision, so make sure you spend time on making sure you are happy with your choice.
-   Universities are different and the same course can be really different at each university, so take the choice of university seriously.
-   Work experience, placements and volunteering don't have to be numerous - quality over quantity.
-   Focus on what you enjoy when you are choosing your subject and don't feel pressured to map out everything before you apply; take one step at a time.
-   There is no such thing as a 'perfect application.' Everyone has had different experiences and different reasons as to why they want to study a given subject, and that inherently means that everyone's applications will be different.

Things I wish I had known as I was applying:

- Try not to stress too much about it; the process can be very full on, especially alongside schoolwork, so make sure you make time to relax too.
- One small step each day will go a long way towards breaking up the application process and making it more manageable.
- If you are really keen to do something, it is not a failure to re-apply.
- For interviews, be friendly to your interviewers and to other applicants. It will help make everyone's day a lot better, and interviewers will look for students that they would enjoy teaching.
- Get everything done comfortably before the deadline.
- It's OK (and the right thing) to dedicate a lot of time to the application process and let your A-Levels take a back seat for a little while; don't worry, this is completely normal!
- Treat the interview like a conversation rather than a debate and take a moment (and a breath) before answering questions.
- Do preparation on topics you find interesting, rather than because you think you should.
- Talk to people who are currently studying your dream subject - they will be happy to help.
- Be prepared to go through many, many drafts of your personal statement until the final version flows properly and fully represents the reasons why you want to study your chosen subject.

Things I wish I had known when I was accepted and started my Degree:

- Try to stay on top of your course from day I – it's much easier to maintain than it is to catch-up.
- Try out at least a couple of societies, both things you know you enjoy and things that sound like they might be fun. Get involved!
- Try to get out of the student bubble once in a while.
- Build a good relationship with your lecturers.
- University work is nothing like A-level work. You will need to learn 'how to learn' all over again.
- Key A-level subjects are highly relevant and shouldn't be so easily forgotten.
- No matter what social/economic background you are from and how it compares to the predominant background at your university or College, when it comes down it you are there for academic work and learning - so don't be intimidated by any of it.
- Speak up, especially in supervisions.
- Lectures are important for giving an overview of different topics – without them, readings become more tedious and difficult to deal with.
- Different supervisors will have different opinions of your writing style - you can't please everyone.
- Don't pressure yourself early on, it takes time to adapt.

Your Reading List

Paperback Books

Title	Notes
Alexander Dewdney: *The New Turing Omnibus,* 2003	**Outline:** Contains a selection of articles focused on computer science theory and its applications. Many diagrams and example questions are provided to test the reader's understanding of the content. The topics are varied and cover many areas of computer science – which gives readers a solid foundation in the field.
	Main learning points: General discussion of algorithms, both computable and non-computable types, and includes sections on Newton-Raphson method, neural networks, computer viruses, Mandelbrot set and many more.
	ISBN: 978-0805071665
Charles Petzold: *Code: The Hidden Language of Computer Hardware and Software,* 2000	**Outline:** Introduces the concept of binary mathematics clearly and illustratively. Starting from these fundamentals, it discusses ideas of communication, data/information and logic. Key concepts of computing and programming are covered in an engaging and visual way.
	Main learning points: Covers binary systems and number systems in general. Logic gates and Boolean logic are also discussed – the areas about operations and chipsets can become slightly dull. Its final part discusses programming languages – both high and low level.
	ISBN: 978-0735611313

Subrata Dasgupta: *Computer Science: A Very Short Introduction,* 2016	**Outline:** From the popular *The Very Short Introductions* series from Oxford, this book addresses the theoretical foundations of computer science in a simple and straight-forward way, and helps readers form the conceptual basis for the subject of computer science.
	Main learning points: Focuses on fundamental ideas such as algorithms and programming, but eventually progresses onto more developed and modern concepts of computer science, such as artificial intelligence, cognitive modelling and biological computing.
	ISBN: 978-0198733461
Brian Christian, Tom Griffiths: *Algorithms to Live By: The Computer Science of Human Decisions,* 2016	**Outline:** Very interesting text that marries computer algorithms and the daily lives of humans. Encourages the reader to think critically about the choices they make on a daily basis and introduces them to improved methods for these everyday tasks by adopting methods used by computers instead.
	Main learning points: Includes many common decision-making dilemmas and discusses the contrasting ways in which humans and computers might tackle them. Provides an alternative view for approaching problems and provides practical, simple solutions.
	ISBN: 978-0007547999

John D. Kelleher, Brendan Tierney: *Data Science,* 2018	**Outline:** More of an extra-curricular read, but definitely worthwhile for those interested in storing and analysing data. It's from the *MIT Press Essential Knowledge Series* and covers the fundamental ideas regarding data science; from the history of the field, through primary data concepts and onto data infrastructure.
	Main learning points: Covers fundamental concepts of data and outlines the stages of a project in data science. Discusses the basics of machine learning and the ethical, legal and moral issues regarding data science. Finishes off with future prospects and impacts of the field.
	ISBN: 978-1469070834
Martin Lewinter, Jeanine Meyer: *Elementary Number Theory with Programming,* 2015	**Outline:** Bridges the gap between number theory and programming. Provides many example questions and solutions. Suitable for readers from a range of backgrounds – no previous experience of programming is necessary as all fundamental concepts are addressed.
	Main learning points: General number theory; begins with more elementary ideas such as Pascal's triangle, primes and modular arithmetic, and develops onto more complicated ideas such as sums and partitions, Euler Phi-function and number-theoretic functions.
	ISBN: 978-1119062769

Marcus Du Sautoy: *The Creativity Code: How AI is learning to write, paint and think,* 2019	**Outline:** Also more of a topical read, but incredibly interesting for those curious about artificial intelligence. Relates the field of computer science to the arts, whilst also informing the reader of the deep links to mathematics.
	Main learning points: Explains the mathematical nature and rules of algorithms; mathematical disciplines of group theory and symmetry are briefly discussed. The subjectivity of art is explored and the distinction between randomness and 'good' art is analyzed. Future of artificial intelligence is also discussed.
	ISBN: 978-0674988132
J. Glenn Brookshear: *Computer Science: An Overview,* 2008	**Outline:** A complete overview of the field of computer science for readers of all levels of experience. Contains the fundamental topics as well as modern ones to create a full discussion of the subject.
	Main learning points: Basic topics such as data storage/representation, machine language and architecture are covered in this book. There is in-depth discussion of both fundamental hardware and software topics; although the software topics are language-independent to emphasize the important ideas of programming, as opposed to the syntax. In later chapters, relevant and current topics such as artificial intelligence and bioinformatics are discussed.
	ISBN: 978-0321544285

Journals

Name	Notes
CS4FN	'Computer Science For Fun' – a magazine about research in computer science aimed at students.
Algorithmica	A scientific journal based on the research and application of computer algorithms.
BBC's 'Make It Digital'	A major UK initiative focused on inspiring young people to get creative with coding and digital technology.

Online Resources

Link	Notes
https://projecteuler.net/	A wide array of challenging programming problems of a mathematical nature. This website is for anyone interested in mathematics, logic and problem-solving.
https://www.codecademy.com/	Free online coding lessons for a range of languages, as well as for SQL and web development.
https://nrich.maths.org/frontpage	A collection of maths problems and resources for learners of all ages. Helpful for developing problem-solving skills and preparing for STEP.
https://www.ukmt.org.uk/	Hosts many competitions for maths and problem-solving – papers are available online for many different levels of mathematical ability.
https://artofproblemsolving.com/resources	Includes a large variety of resources, such as videos and online interactive systems. It even gives you the chance to work on a research project with a mentor.

http://www.alice.org/	Helpful introduction to object-oriented programming; it is a block-based programming environment which can be used to make simple games in 3D and animations.
https://www.olympiad.org.uk/	Website of the national computing competition – includes challenging programming problems.
http://www.maths.ox.ac.uk/about-us/life-oxford-mathematics/oxford-mathematics-alphabet	An A-Z of current areas of research in the field of mathematics. Explained in an accessible way, this is a useful tool for getting up-to-date with the recent research in the subject.
https://www.numberphile.com/	Includes podcasts, articles and videos based on mathematics and its applications. Very informative and engaging, with visual methods of teaching.
http://www.cs.ox.ac.uk/geomlab/	Guided activities which illustrate key concepts in programming and are interactive.

http://www.philocomp.net/ai/elizabeth.htm	Elizabeth is a natural language processing program. This is an entertaining application of artificial intelligence which provides an introduction to natural language processing.
https://www.turtle.ox.ac.uk/	A graphics programming environment which is programmed in Java syntax.

Work Experience

What's the point of work experience?

Arranging work experience is a vital step in demonstrating your passion for a subject, as unless you're going to become an academic (and even if you think you are, very few people ever actually do), you'll be using your degree out in the wide world of work in just a few years' time.

It is really important that you have at least some sense of how Computer Science is used in the real world; both for your application, and for you to make sure that you actually want to study the subject. You wouldn't want to apply for Law and spend three years studying Law, only to discover you can't stand being a lawyer; you would never really get the full value out of your degree. The chances of that happening if you've already gained experience as a solicitor, a data analyst, or a market researcher are much smaller.

You'll find it much easier to explain why you want to study Computer Science once you have real-world context for it; this will help you make your Personal Statement more persuasive and help in the interview as well. It's much more convincing to say you're interested in molecular biophysics after you've spent a week working in a pharmaceutical lab than when you've simply thought about it.

Applying for work experience can be a little tricky though, particularly if you don't know very much about an industry, or anyone who already works in it. We aren't all lucky enough to be able to ask an uncle or an aunt, especially in more niche industries or those that are mainly based in London.

Who should I contact to arrange work experience?

To arrange work experience, first of all you need to work out what industry you want to try out. In any industry, there will be a few big companies that you've already heard of, and many of them will already have work experience programmes in place. These big organisations are the easiest to apply to, which often means that they're the most popular, and the hardest to get into.

For example, if you want to do work experience at the BBC, you have to apply four months in advance, and then they only have a very limited number of openings for under 18s. Plus, everyone has heard of the BBC, so anyone who's looking to get into the media is going to apply for work experience with them by default, making for fierce competition.

Smaller organisations, like an independent TV production company, are harder to find, and may not have a formal work experience programme in place. However, these are often the best places to do work experience; a smaller organisation will not only have fewer applicants, but also be more likely to give you useful experiences. If you're suddenly one of eight people working on a project, you're much more likely to be given real responsibilities and something interesting to do than you are if you're working with a team of two hundred people.

The best way to find these smaller companies is to start local. Use a search engine to investigate what companies there are nearby in the sector you're interested in.

Smaller local companies might not be as prestigious as the BBC, but the point of work experience is to find out what working in an industry is like, which means actually getting to do some work – not just photocopying and fetching coffees. And you have a much better chance of that if you look small and local instead of just big, famous, and in London.

What should I say when asking for work experience?

To make things even easier for you, overleaf is a template for an email you can send when trying to arrange work experience. Most companies will have a generic info@company.com email address you can write to, but it is always worth trying LinkedIn to find a specific contact. Someone in Human Resources is normally a good bet.

Think about who is likely to read your email – there's no point in emailing the CEO if they never read it! You're also more likely to get through and get a reply if you know the name of the person who you're trying to contact; so try to address a particular person rather than just writing 'Dear Sir/Madam'.

You want to give the reader some background as to who you are, so they can understand why you want work experience, so be sure to introduce yourself as well as asking politely. Particularly for smaller companies, you want to make sure that you're offering them something, not just asking for them to do you a favour; highlight what you're good at, and how you can make yourself useful. Nothing too ambitious though! If you tell them that you can run the company, or that you're already an expert, you'll come across as arrogant and lacking in self-awareness, which won't help your case.

Mailto: Laura@businesscompany.co.uk
Subject: Work Experience Enquiry
Dear Laura Laurason,

I hope you're well. My name is David Davidson, and I am writing to you as I would like to arrange work experience with your software company. I'm currently studying for my A levels at [Local Sixth Form College], and am hoping to apply to Cambridge next year to study Computer Science.

I'm very keen to work as a [programmer] once I graduate, and would appreciate being able to find out what computer science is really like by spending a few days with your company.

I already have experience working with Excel, and would be happy to take on any tasks you might have around the practice. I'm free for the whole of the summer holidays (DD/MM to DD/MM) and have my own transport to and from your office.

Thank you for reading, and I hope to hear back from you soon.

Thanks,
David Davidson

Study Strategies

This is a short extract taken from The Ultimate Guide to Exam Success, which offers a comprehensive plan for optimising your study strategies.

The 8 Principles of Exam Success

The 8 Principles focus on what we aren't taught at school about exams – namely, how to actually master the process of preparing for and performing optimally in our exams, while maintaining a healthy mental and physical state.

The 8 Principles of Exam Success are split into 2 groups:

- Optimising The Studying Process
- Optimising The Studying Lifestyle

Each of the 2 groups is composed of 4 Principles.

The areas that we need to optimise as part of our Studying Process include:

1. **Time-Management** – effective prioritisation and planning techniques to increase productivity and reduce procrastination.
2. **Study Tools & Techniques** – optimising how, where and when we study.
3. **Mind-set Management** – understanding the sources of our anxiety, low motivation and doubt, and using 8 different tools to address, manage and resolve them.
4. **On-The-Day Performance** – tactics to implement immediately before, during and after the exam.

However, we can't allow ourselves to become consumed with the Studying Process to the extent where we feel that focusing on it alone will allow us to excel in our exams. We must recognise that the overall effectiveness of our study process is significantly impacted by the lifestyle choices that we make during this time.

The areas that we need to optimise as part of our Studying Lifestyle include:

5. **Physical Activity & Movement** – the amount of physical activity and movement in our day.
6. **Nutrition & Hydration** – the quality of our nutrition and the importance of staying well-hydrated.
7. **Sleep** – optimising the quality and quantity of sleep we get per day.
8. **Support Group** – the academic and personal support groups that we have access to.

After all, every one of us has been told countless times about the importance of getting enough sleep, drinking lots of water and doing exercise. But for some of us, it becomes easier to convince ourselves to actually act on these once we understand the basic science behind them, or appreciate that there is real evidence proving their benefits.

UCAS Reference

Why does the UCAS Reference Matter?

The UCAS reference is the most underrated part of the university application, and is where the gap between a well prepared school, with experience of the Cambridge process, and a school coming to it for the first time, shows the most.

Schools with experience of the process will know what aspects of an applicant's work to highlight, how to frame their achievements relative to their peers, and what things to prioritise for each course.

Without the context of past admissions success, it can be hard for a referee to put forward the best and most convincing case for an applicant.

The reference is considered very important by Cambridge, but often receives far less attention than the Personal Statement, for example. This is because, conventionally, one teacher will be writing upwards of twenty or thirty references, while each student is only writing their own personal statement over the course of a series of drafts.

It would of course be ludicrous to ask a teacher to write the equivalent of thirty personal statements over their summer holiday; before redrafting them, editing them, and then rewriting them again to fit perfectly to every student's choice of university.

This is why we encourage applicants to collaborate with their teachers on their references – even if it is a little awkward – to identify the key message they want to put across to universities; making sure that they have the right predicted grades, the right contexts provided for their achievements so far, and their relevant skills highlighted.

As educators themselves, university admissions tutors take the opinions of other educational professionals very seriously, so making sure your reference is complete and accurate is crucial to your application.

How to write a great UCAS reference

University admissions tutors know what they're doing; they'll find it very easy to spot a template, or any other kind of copy/paste going on. This means that working in collaboration with your teachers can really improve your reference, as admissions tutors will be looking closely for references that go into real detail.

To make things as straightforward as possible, we've created a checklist for the UCAS Reference that you can fill out in collaboration with your teacher. The best thing to do is to make sure that you cover the following key points in the reference, giving real examples for each.

- Academic performance and potential.
- Suitability, motivation, and commitment.
- Relevant skills and personal qualities.
- Recent achievements, particularly in relevant subject areas.
- Relevant work experience or enrichment activities.
- Any contextual information which might warrant special consideration.
- Any mitigating factors which might affect performance.

And remember not to repeat yourself; if you've mentioned grade eight piano in your form, it doesn't need to be in your Personal Statement - and it doesn't need to be in here either!

Your Letter of Recommendation

In addition to your UCAS Reference, it can be helpful to reach out directly to the college; making your case for a place with more detail and subtlety than the UCAS form will allow. To make things as straightforward as possible, we've created a template for the Letter of Recommendation that you can fill out in collaboration with your teacher.

This template needs to be sent to the Head of Admissions at the college where you're applying to study. We have filled out as much of the content as we possibly can, so all you need to ask your referee do is fill in the following fields accordingly:

- Addressee Name
- Addressee Address
- Student Name
- Name of University/College
- Number of years you've known the student
- Your position in relation to the student
- Pronouns: his/her/theirs or he/she/they
- Subject they're studying
- One piece of relevant work

We hope this makes the recommendation process much simpler for all involved. Of course, you can customise the letter as much as you want, but this should give you everything you need to start.

Printed on School Letterhead

Letter of Recommendation for John Smith

[Addressee Name & Address]

YOUR SCHOOL
LOGO HERE

Dear **[Addressee Name]**,

It is my pleasure to recommend **[Name of student]** for admission to **[Name of university]**. I have known **[Name of student]** for **[x years]** in my capacity as **[his/her/their]** **[your position to the student]** at **[school name]**. During that time, I've seen **[Student name]** grow into an outstanding individual, both academically and personally.

[Student name] has shown a great interest in **[subject]** for as long as I have known them. Their enthusiasm and passion towards **[subject]** is demonstrated through **[example of work student has done]** which was completed to a very high standard and beyond the capability of most of their peers. This drive to succeed is evident in every academic foray **[student name]** has undertaken.

I believe, with the support of **[name of university]**'s highly regarded **[subject]** course, **[student name]** will be able to translate this passion to a very bright future. The high calibre of students that **[student name]** would be around at **[name of university]** would bring out the best in **[him/her/them]**, as I am sure **[student name]** would help bring out in each of them.

[Student name]'s enthusiasm and determination has made **[him/her/them]** a highly regarded student at our **[school]**, popular amongst both teachers and students. **[He/she/they]** has a smile for everyone and strives to be a positive influence on those around **[him/her/them]**.

(continued overleaf – do not include this comment in your letter)

[Student name] is unquestionably an exceptional candidate to study at your prestigious university. **[He/she/they]** is an extremely bright student with an extraordinarily positive attitude towards **[his/her/their]** work. I am confident **[student name]** will quickly become a valued member at **[name of university]**.

I unreservedly recommend them to you.

Please feel free to contact me if you have any questions about **[Student name]**.

Sincerely,

[Your Signature]
[Your Name]
[Your Position]
[School Name]

Final Thoughts

A message from founder, Dr Rohan Agarwal.

This guide is your companion through every stage of your application process. Make sure you are not too hard on yourself if you fall behind at any point, but do make sure that you catch up as soon as possible.

Cambridge isn't a mythical place, it's an achievable reality, through preparation and commitment to your decision to study there. If you find yourself deviating away from it, it's time to re-assess how much you really do want it!

Remember that the route to success is your approach and practice. Don't fall into the trap that "you can't prepare for the test/interview"– this could not be further from the truth. With targeted preparation and focused reading, you can dramatically boost your chances of getting that dream offer.

Work hard, never give up, and do yourself justice.

Good luck!

Dr Rohan Agarwal

Made in the USA
Middletown, DE
12 March 2022

62531458R00056